Troodon

by Daniel Cohen

Consultant:
Larry Dean Martin, Ph.D.
Professor-Senior Curator
Natural History Museum and Biodiversity Research Center
University of Kansas, Lawrence, Kansas

Bridgestone Books
an imprint of Capstone Press
Mankato, Minnesota

Bridgestone Books are published by Capstone Press
151 Good Counsel Drive, P.O. Box 669, Mankato, Minnesota 56002
www.capstonepress.com

Library of Congress Cataloging-in-Publication Data
Cohen, Daniel, 1936–
    Troodon / by Daniel Cohen.
        p. cm.—(Discovering dinosaurs)
    Summary: Briefly describes how this dinosaur looked, what it ate, where it lived, and how
scientists learned about it.
    Includes bibliographical references and index.
    ISBN 0-7368-2527-4 (hardcover)
    1. Troodon—Juvenile literature. [1. Troodon. 2. Dinosaurs.] I. Title. II. Series.
QE862.S3C5647 2004
567.914—dc22   2003015687

Editorial Credits
Amanda Doering, editor; Linda Clavel, series designer; Enoch Peterson, book designer and
    illustrator; Alta Schaffer, photo researcher; Karen Risch, product planning editor

Photo Credits
Museum of the Rockies, cover, 1, 10–11, 16–17
The Natural History Museum/J. Sibbick, 20; Orbis, 4, 8, 12, 14
OSF, 6

1 2 3 4 5 6 09 08 07 06 05 04

Table of Contents

Troodon compared to a
5-foot (1.5-meter) tall human

Troodon

Troodon (TROH-oh-don) was a small, fast-moving **dinosaur**. It lived until about 65 million years ago. Troodon was only 6 feet (1.8 meters) long. It weighed about 100 pounds (45 kilograms). Troodon means "wounding tooth."

The World of Troodon

Troodon lived in what is now North America. Earth was different during troodon's time. The climate was warmer and wetter than it is today.

climate
the usual weather in a place

Saurornithoides

Relatives of Troodon

Troodon belonged to a group of small meat-eating dinosaurs called troodontidae (TROH-oh-don-TIH-day). Saurornithoides (sore-OR-nith-OID-eez) was a relative of troodon. These dinosaurs moved quickly. They were also good hunters.

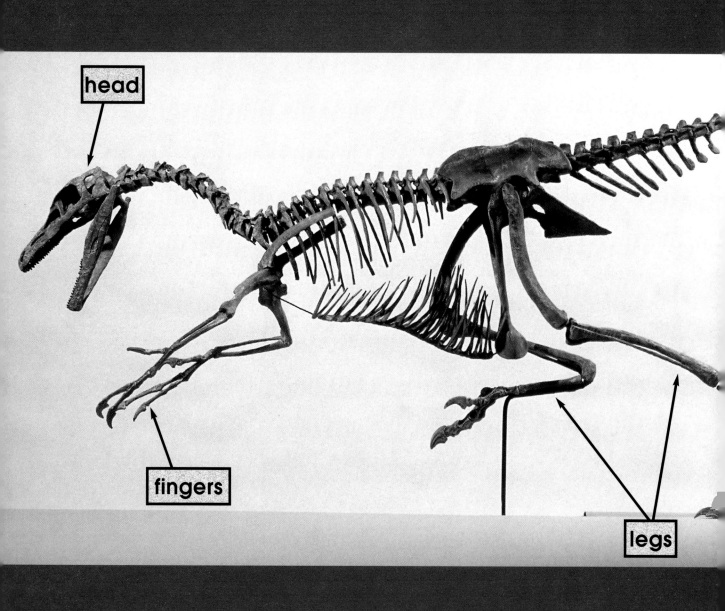

head

fingers

legs

Parts of Troodon

Troodon was small, but very powerful. It walked on thin, strong back legs. Troodon grasped its prey with long, thin fingers. It used its tail to **balance** its body. Troodon had about 120 sharp teeth to rip apart its food. It also had large eyes for a dinosaur.

prey
an animal that is hunted and eaten for food

11

Eyes for the Hunt

Troodon's eyes made it a good predator. Most night hunters have large eyes like troodon had. **Scientists** believe troodon hunted at night. Troodon's eyes faced forward like a human's eyes. Troodon could see things in front of it without turning its head.

predator
an animal that hunts and eats other animals

What Troodon Ate

Troodon was a **carnivore**, meaning it ate meat. Troodon's speed allowed it to catch small, quick animals. Troodon may have hunted in packs. It probably ate small dinosaurs, lizards, and small mammals. It may have also eaten the eggs of larger dinosaurs.

mammal
a warm-blooded animal with a backbone

The End of Troodon

Troodon lived until about 65 million years ago. At that time, all dinosaurs died out. No one is sure why the dinosaurs became **extinct**. Scientists think a meteorite from space hit Earth. Effects from the meteorite may have killed the dinosaurs.

meteorite
a rock that falls from space to Earth

17

Discovering Troodon

In 1855, Ferdinand V. Hayden found the first **fossils** of troodon in Montana. Later, more fossils were found in Alberta, Canada. These fossils were thought to be a new dinosaur. More than 50 years later, scientists learned that the fossils were from troodon.

Studying Troodon Today

Scientists once thought all dinosaurs were large, slow, and stupid. By studying troodon, scientists learned that this idea was not true. Troodon was a small, quick dinosaur. It had a large brain for its size. Today, scientists think that troodon was Earth's smartest dinosaur.

Hands On: Smart Dinosaur

Scientists can tell how smart dinosaurs were by comparing their brain size to their body size. A larger brain in a small body meant the dinosaur was smarter than a large dinosaur with a small brain. Try this activity to see which was a smarter dinosaur.

What You Need

tape
tape measure
avocado pit
walnut

What You Do

1. Place a piece of tape on the floor or ground. With the tape measure and another piece of tape, mark out 6 feet (1.8 meters). Troodon was 6 feet (1.8 meters) long.
2. Next to troodon's measurement, mark out 30 feet (9 meters) with tape. Stegosaurus was 30 feet (9 meters) long. How many times longer was stegosaurus than troodon?
3. Stegosaurus also weighed about 8,000 pounds (3,600 kilograms). Troodon weighed only 100 pounds (45 kilograms). How much more did stegosaurus weigh than troodon?
4. With the tape measure, measure the avocado pit and the walnut. The avocado pit is the size of troodon's brain. The walnut is the size of stegosaurus' brain. Which is bigger? Which do you think was the smarter dinosaur?

Glossary

balance (BAL-uhnss)—to try to keep steady without falling

carnivore (KAR-nuh-vor)—an animal that eats only meat

dinosaur (DYE-na-sore)—an extinct land reptile; dinosaurs lived on Earth for at least 150 million years.

extinct (ek-STINGT)—no longer living anywhere in the world

fossil (FOSS-uhl)—the remains or traces of something that once lived; bones and footprints can be fossils.

scientist (SYE-uhn-tist)—a person who studies the world around us

Read More

Devillier, Christy. *Troodon.* Dinosaurs. Edina, Minn.: Abdo, 2004.

Matthews, Rupert. *Troodon.* Gone Forever! Chicago: Heinemann, 2004.

Internet Sites

FactHound offers a safe, fun way to find Internet sites related to this book. All of the sites on FactHound have been researched by our staff.

Here's how:
1. Visit *www.facthound.com*
2. Type in this special code **0736825274** for age-appropriate sites. Or enter a search word related to this book for a more general search.
3. Click on the **Fetch It** button.

FactHound will fetch the best sites for you!

Index